Start TO Finish
Second Series

FROM Shoot TO Apple

STACY TAUS-BOLSTAD

LERNER PUBLICATIONS · Minneapolis

Photo Acknowledgments

The images in this book are used with the permission of: © AgStock Images/John Marshall, pp. 1, 5; © Evgeny Karandaev/Shutterstock Images, p. 3; © AgStock Images/Jim Stephenson, p. 7; © Max Baumann/Shutterstock Images, p. 9; © Rainer/Dreamstime.com, p. 11; © Terhox/Dreamstime.com, p. 13; © Doug Matthews/Shutterstock Images, p. 15; © Mazzzur/Shutterstock Images, p. 17; © Inc/Shutterstock Images, p. 19; © Jupiterimages/FoodPix/Getty Images, p. 21; © Todd Strand/Independent Picture Service, p. 23.

Front cover: iStockphoto.com/Murphy_Shewchuk.

Lerner Publications Company
A division of Lerner Publishing Group, Inc.
241 First Avenue North
Minneapolis, MN 55401 USA

For reading levels and more information, look up this title at www.lernerbooks.com.

Main body text set in Arta Std Book 20/26.
Typeface provided by International Typeface Corp.

Library of Congress Cataloging-in-Publication Data

Taus-Bolstad, Stacy.
        From shoot to apple / by Stacy Taus-Bolstad.
            p.   cm. — (Start to finish, second series: nature's cycles)
        Includes index.
        ISBN 978–0–7613–7734–4 (lib. bdg. : alk. paper)
        ISBN 978–0–7613–8835–7 (EB pdf)
        1. Apples—Juvenile literature. I. Title.
SB363.T294 2012
634'.11—dc23   2011024571

Manufactured in the United States of America
5–42547–12216–7/13/2016

TABLE OF Contents

A farmer starts a new tree.	4
The shoots and the trunk grow.	6
The tree gets big.	8
Flowers open.	10
The flowers fall.	12
The apples grow.	14
The apples change.	16
Workers pick the apples.	18
People buy the apples.	20
Crunch!	22
Glossary	24
Index	24

Yum! An apple! How does it grow?

A farmer starts a new tree.

A farmer uses parts of two apple trees to start a new tree. The farmer joins small branches from a grown tree to the trunk of a young tree. The branches are called **shoots**.

The shoots and the trunk grow.

The farmer covers the shoots and the trunk with wax to keep them healthy. The shoots and the trunk grow together into a new tree. This tree will make tasty apples.

The tree gets big.

The tree gets taller. Branches grow from the trunk. Leaves grow from the branches.

Flowers open.

When the tree is about three years old, it begins to grow flowers. Flowers **bloom** from the branches each spring.

11

The flowers fall.

The flower petals fall to the ground in late spring. Tiny new apples are left behind. The new apples are green.

The apples grow.

Young apples are too sour to eat. Water and sunlight help them to grow bigger and sweeter.

The apples change.

The apples become **ripe**. Some kinds of apples turn red or yellow. Others stay green. Ripe apples are juicy and sweet.

Workers pick the apples.

Apples are ripe in late summer or early fall.
It is time for workers to pick them from the tree.
Apples are usually picked by hand. Workers
use ladders to pick apples at the top of the tree.

People buy the apples.

Trucks take the apples to be sold. These people are buying apples at an apple stand. Many people buy apples at grocery stores.

Crunch!

Take a bite. This juicy fruit has grown from shoot to apple.

Glossary

bloom (BLOOM): open up

ripe (RYP): ready to pick from a tree

shoots (SHOOTS): small branches from a tree

Index

apple tree, 4, 6, 8, 10, 18

buying, 20

flowers, 10, 12

picking, 18

shoots, 4, 6, 22
sunlight, 14

water, 14